AFRICA FOCUS

ANCIENT AFRICA

Rob Bowden and Rosie Wilson

Heinemann Library
Chicago, Illinois

www.heinemannraintree.com
Visit our website to find out more information about Heinemann-Raintree books.

To order:
☎ Phone 888-454-2279
💻 Visit www.heinemannraintree.com to browse our catalog and order online.

©2010 Heinemann Library
an imprint of Capstone Global Library, LLC
Chicago, Illinois

Edited by Louise Galpine and Rachel Howells
Designed by Richard Parker and Manhattan Design
Original illustrations © Capstone Global Library Ltd
Illustrated by Oxford Designers and Illustrators
Picture research by Mica Brancic
Originated by Heinemann Library
Printed and bound in the United States by Corporate Graphics.

14 13 12 11 10
10 9 8 7 6 5 4 3 2

Library of Congress Cataloging-in-Publication Data
Bowden, Rob, 1973-
  Ancient Africa / Rob Bowden and Rosie Wilson.
    p. cm. -- (Africa focus)
  Includes bibliographical references and index.
  ISBN 978-1-4329-2439-3 (hc) -- ISBN 978-1-4329-2444-7
(pb)
  1. Africa--History. I. Wilson, Rosie. II. Title.
  DT20.B69 2008
  960--dc22
                        2008048306

  062010
  005798RP

Acknowledgments

We would like to thank the following for permission to reproduce photographs: akg-images p. **40**; Corbis pp. **10 & 14** (© The Gallery Collection), **13** (Robert Harding World Imagery/1996-98/AccuSoft Inc., All Rights), **23** (© Tim Graham), **26** (Werner Forman), **27** (Sergio Pitamitz/zefa), **35** (Bojan Brecelj), **39** (© Corbis); EASI-Images pp. **25 & 29** (Roy Maconachie); Getty Images pp. **5** (Hulton Archive/Stringer), **7** (Melville B. Grosvenor/National Geographic), **15** (Robert Harding World Imagery/Andrew McConnell), **31** (Photographer's Choice/Sylvain Grandadam), **32** (Time Life Pictures/Mansell/Time Life Pictures), **33** (Henry Guttmann/Stringer/Hulton Archive), **41** (Hulton Archive/Stringer Collection); Library of Congress p. **38**; Lonely Planet Images p. **20** (Ariadne Van Zandbergen); Photolibrary pp. **4** (Phototake Science/Carolina Biological Supply Company), **8** (John Warburton-Lee Photography/Susanna Wyatt), **9** (Oxford Scientific/Ariadne Van Zandbergen), **18** (JTB Photo), **30** (John Warburton-Lee Photography/Nigel Pavitt); The Bridgeman Art Library p. **37**.

Cover photograph of bronze head, Benin, reproduced with permission of Corbis (Christie's Images).

We would like to thank Danny Block for his invaluable help in the preparation of this book.

Every effort has been made to contact copyright holders of material reproduced in this book. Any omissions will be rectified in subsequent printings if notice is given to the publishers.

Contents

Some words are printed in bold, **like this**. You can find out what they mean by looking in the glossary on page 44.

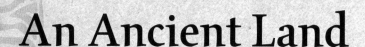

An Ancient Land

The study of ancient humans looks at how people lived in the distant past. Our human **ancestors** were living in Africa more than 1.6 million years ago! In fact, scientists believe that human life began in Africa. This is why the ancient history of Africa is in some ways the ancient history of us all. Our first ancestors lived **primitive** lives, but Africa also holds the secrets of early societies that were rich and highly organized. We know this because of treasures and objects that were left behind. **Fossils**, bones, tools, and art have been found across the African **continent**.

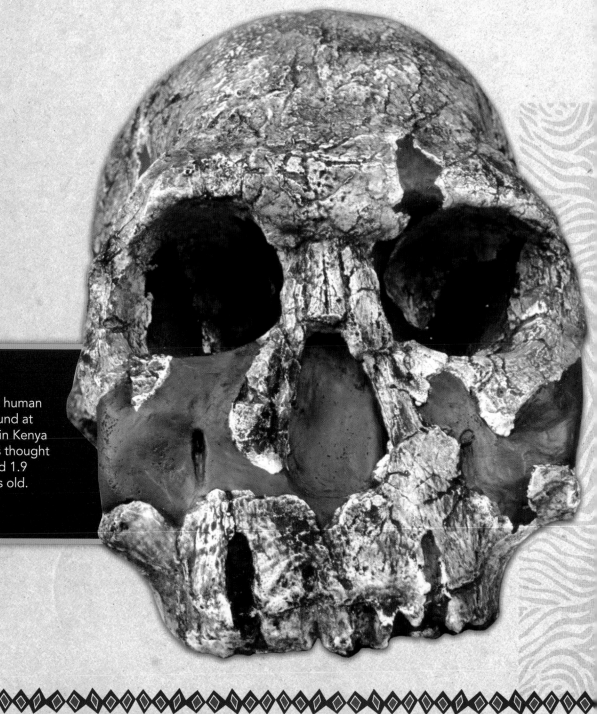

This ancient human skull was found at Koobi Fora in Kenya in 1972. It is thought to be around 1.9 million years old.

This group of African slaves was chained together and guarded by a soldier in Tanzania in 1896.

Great societies

Africa has seen the rise and fall of many great societies. They grew strong by using or trading the continent's rich **resources**. These included gold, salt, and **ivory**. Many of Africa's people were also traded—as **slaves**. Crafts and skills, including farming, carpentry, and metalwork, were developed by early African societies. They may be long gone now, but in parts of Africa you can still see evidence of how these societies might have lived.

Africa and the world

About 500 years ago, explorers and traders from Europe began to travel to Africa. They returned to Europe with stories of Africa's rich resources and opportunities for **trade**. Powerful European countries sent more explorers and even armies to Africa. They brought gold, spices, and other fascinating items back to Europe. They also took people as slaves and shipped them to work in the Americas. Millions of people were taken as slaves and African societies suffered greatly. Slavery eventually ended in the 19th century, but by then Africa had been weakened and was under the control of European countries.

The Origin of Humankind

All living things on Earth are given a scientific name. This allows us to see how different **species** are related and how they develop over time. Modern humans, like you and I, are known scientifically as *Homo sapiens sapiens*. Modern humans first appeared around 170,000 years ago in eastern or southern Africa. Earlier human **ancestors** had already been living in Africa, Europe, and Asia, but *Homo sapiens sapiens* gradually replaced them. They spread from Africa across Asia and Europe, and eventually reached the Americas, Australia, and even remote islands.

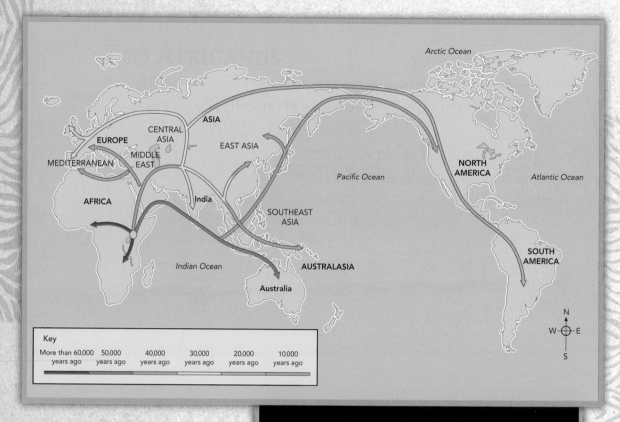

This map shows how humankind first spread across the world from Africa.

Twenty-first century science

Every human has a unique biological code that makes him or her slightly different from all other humans. We call this code **DNA**. Scientists have used DNA as another way to discover the starting point of humankind. This is made possible because parts of our DNA are only passed from mothers to their children. Scientists can follow these parts back for thousands of years. In this way they have shown that modern humans all came from the same original DNA around 171,500 years ago. This is about the time the first modern humans are thought to have lived in Africa.

Mary Leakey (left) carefully removes a fossil from a cliff at Olduvai Gorge in Tanzania in 1965.

THE LEAKEY FAMILY

Mary and Louis Leakey made important discoveries of ancient human life in eastern Africa. In 1959 they found ancient remains in Olduvai Gorge in Tanzania. The remains helped scientists figure out when modern humans first appeared. Mary also found fossilized footprints that showed how our ancestors learned to walk about 3.5 million years ago. Their son Richard and his wife Meave have continued this work. In 1967 Richard found ancient remains at Koobi Fora in northern Kenya. Meave and their daughter Louise Leakey are still exploring the Koobi Fora region today.

Getting brainier

As our ancestors **evolved** into modern humans, they became more intelligent. At the same time, their brains got bigger. Scientists believe this is a direct link—the bigger the brain, the smarter they were! One way to see how intelligent people were millions of years ago is to look at the design of the tools they were using. For example, simple tools such as sticks used for digging developed into shaped tools such as small axes or picks. Stone was used instead of wood. Sharpened stone flakes acted as early knives to cut meat.

Hunter-gatherers

Early humans lived by hunting and gathering. Animal bones and seeds that show this way of life have been found alongside ancient human remains. Weapons such as spears would have been used for hunting, and knives were used for preparing meat. **Charcoal** found near some remains shows that humans also used fire a very long time ago.

This ancient rock painting was found in the southern Sahara Desert, Libya. It shows hunters carrying bows and arrows.

Bambuti pygmies

The Bambuti have lived in the **rain forest** of the Congo for at least 4,500 years. Their lives are similar to those of our ancient human ancestors. They get their food by hunting, fishing, and gathering. They use nets, spears, and small bows and arrows. Their homes are small beehive-shaped huts made from a frame of sticks and filled in with leaves. These are temporary shelters because the Bambuti move to a new part of the forest each month. They get everything they need from the rain forest. The Bambuti do not have chiefs or leaders. Problems or arguments are solved by general discussion.

The Bambuti are pygmies, which means they are shorter than the average human. On average they grow no taller than 4 feet 6 inches (137 centimeters).

This Bambuti pygmy is a hunter-gatherer from the village of Ntandi in Uganda.

Early Civilization

Africa was home to one of the world's most famous ancient **civilizations**. The ancient Egyptians were ruled by powerful Egyptian kings called **pharaohs** and were a highly developed society. They lived around the floodplains of the River Nile between around 3000 BCE and 670 BCE. The floodplains provided the ancient Egyptians with **fertile** soils and easy access to water. They developed new technology that allowed them to use the water for growing **crops**. This is known as **irrigation** and was not used by other human societies until much later.

Daily life

Most ancient Egyptians were farmers. They lived in small mud huts and grew cereal crops such as barley and wheat, as well as some vegetables and fruit. The fertile soils meant that they produced more than enough food to meet their own needs. The rest was given to the pharaoh as a form of **tax** and gathered into huge stores. Fishing and hunting were another way that people got food. Many birds **migrated** along the Nile and could be trapped. Deer were also hunted, though normally only by the rich.

Kings of Egypt

Egyptian kings, or pharaohs, had absolute rule over their land and people. The best officers would help the pharaoh control the kingdom. They would collect produce from farmers for storage and organize projects such as building irrigation channels. Food was given out in return for work or during times of shortages. Pharaohs were greatly respected and treated as a god on Earth, alongside Ra, the god of the sun, and Osiris, the god of the dead.

This wall painting from around 1500 BCE shows scenes from the different farming seasons of ancient Egypt—one of the world's earliest civilizations.

Africa Fact

Death was important to the ancient Egyptians. They believed dying was part of a journey to the next life. Many people would keep treasured items to be buried with them for this journey.

Ancient Egyptian farmers used animals to help them do the hard work in the fields.

Expert builders

The ancient Egyptians were talented builders. Their skill can be seen in the pyramids at Giza, near Cairo, which show they knew a lot about mathematics and **engineering**. A huge system of organized labor was needed to build them, with thousands of men moving large blocks of stone across the desert. The pyramids were built as royal burial chambers, but were raided by thieves who stole the pharaohs' treasures. Later, Egyptian pharaohs were buried in the "Valley of the Kings." Their **tombs** were dug deep into the surrounding mountains and covered with earth to hide and protect them from thieves.

The secrets of ancient Egypt

In 1922 the tomb of a young pharaoh named Tutankhamen was found. It was located in the Valley of the Kings and had been untouched for almost 3,000 years! The treasures inside included a **chariot**, furniture, weapons, and many jewels. Tutankhamen was only about 18 years old when he died. His body was found inside three coffins, two made of wood and one of solid gold!

Mummification

Mummification was a process used to **preserve** human bodies for their journey into the next life. Only the wealthiest could afford to have their bodies mummified. First, the internal organs such as the lungs, liver, and stomach (but not the heart) were removed and dried out using a salt called natron. The brain was also removed by smashing it with a hook and pulling it through the nose! The empty body was then covered in natron to dry it out for around 40 days. Once dry, the body was washed and the dried organs were put back in. Sawdust or other dry material was used to stuff the body, and oils made the skin look soft and more lifelike again. The body was then carefully wrapped in many layers of linen before being placed in a coffin ready for burial.

This small solid-gold coffin is one of four containers from the tomb of Tutankhamen. The pharaoh's internal organs were placed in them as part of the process of mummification.

13

Hieroglyphics

Events and stories in ancient Egypt were recorded using a system known as **hieroglyphics**. This is where symbols and pictures, called hieroglyphs, are used instead of letters.

The meaning of hieroglyphs remained something of a mystery until 1799, when a black stone with carved writing on it was found at Rosetta in northern Egypt. Known as the Rosetta Stone, the writing on it recorded events from around 200 BCE in Egyptian and Greek. By comparing the Egyptian hieroglyphs with the Greek alphabet, experts were able to figure out what hieroglyphs meant for the first time.

The Rosetta Stone helped experts to unravel the mystery of hieroglyphics and understand more about life in ancient Egypt.

THE ROSETTA STONE

The Kushites and the Egyptians

The lands to the south of ancient Egypt were known as Nubia and were home to another ancient civilization known as the Kushites. They lived alongside the ancient Egyptians from around 3000 BCE. They **traded** gold and other precious **minerals** with the ancient Egyptians in return for grain. From around 2000 BCE, Nubia was directly controlled by the ancient Egyptians, and the Kushites adopted many Egyptian ways of living. They worshipped Egyptian gods and used pyramids to bury the dead, for example.

By around 800 BCE, ancient Egypt had weakened and Kushite leaders began to conquer parts of Egypt. By 715 BCE the Kushites had taken control of all of Egypt, but only ruled for a short time. They were driven out in around 662 BCE by the Assyrians, another ancient civilization from Mesopotamia (part of modern-day Iraq and Turkey). The Kushite civilization returned to Nubia, where it survived for a further 900 years. Its main city was at Meroë. During this time, the Nubians developed their own unique **culture**. For example, their system of writing changed from Egyptian hieroglyphics to the Meroitic alphabet. Eventually, the Kushites were defeated after invasions from neighboring Ethiopia.

The pyramids of Meroë were built as royal burial tombs. Today, they are Sudan's most popular tourist attraction.

Great Kingdoms

Africa has had many great kingdoms, in which a king or leader controlled an entire region and its people. From 1000 BCE until the late 1700s, these kingdoms were important centres of **trade**, crafts and skills, and learning.

Ancient Ghana (around 300–1100 CE)

Ancient Ghana was in what is now Senegal and Mauritania. The people of the kingdom of Ghana were the Soninke. They were brought together by a leader called Dinga Cisse. The **empire** gained wealth by mining and trading in gold. They used camels to transport gold across the Sahara Desert to the Middle East.

The 11th-century geographer Al-Bakri described ancient Ghana as having the richest gold mines in the world. He wrote:

"The King … puts on a high cap decorated with gold and wrapped in a **turban** of fine cotton. He holds an audience in a domed pavilion around which stand ten horses covered with gold-embroidered materials and on his right, are the sons of the … kings of his country, wearing splendid clothes and their hair plaited with gold."

Africa Fact

One thing that ancient Ghana traded for gold was salt. But the salt traders and Ghanaians did not understand each other. To solve this, it is said they used a system of "silent trade." Salt traders would leave salt at an agreed place for the Ghanaian traders to inspect. The Ghanaians would then leave an amount of gold that they were willing to pay. When the salt traders returned, they would count the gold. If they were happy then they would leave their salt and the Ghanaians would take it. If they were unhappy then they would not leave their salt until the Ghanaians left more gold. This unusual silent trade would have needed a great deal of trust!

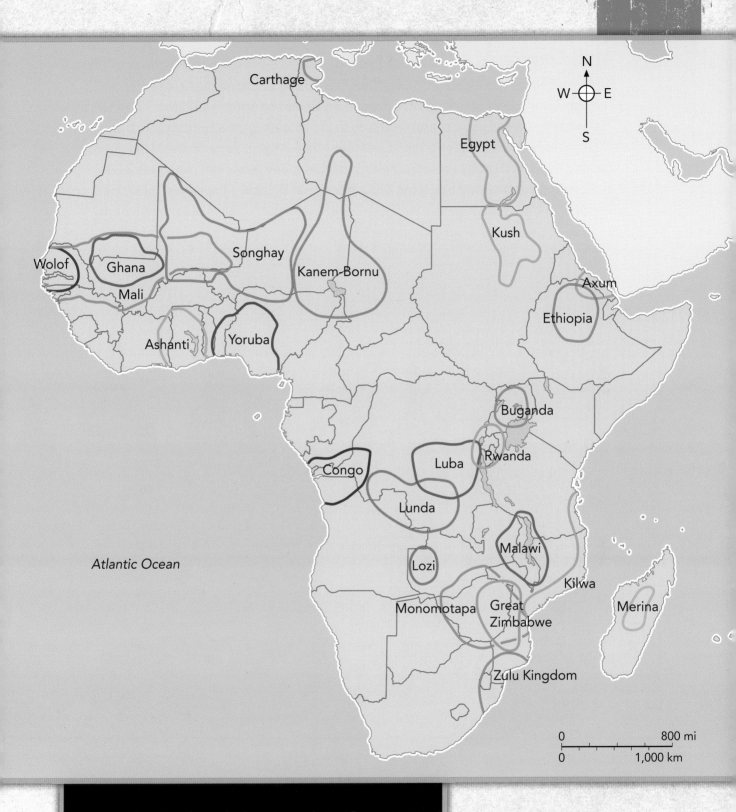

Carthage

Egypt

N
W — E
S

Kush

Wolof

Ghana

Songhay

Kanem-Bornu

Axum

Mali

Ethiopia

Ashanti

Yoruba

Buganda

Congo

Luba

Rwanda

Lunda

Atlantic Ocean

Lozi

Malawi

Kilwa

Monomotapa

Great
Zimbabwe

Merina

Zulu Kingdom

0   800 mi
0   1,000 km

This map shows the location and size of
some of Africa's best-known early kingdoms
and societies. The colored lines show where
the boundaries used to be.

Mali Empire

The Mali Empire was created by a **warrior** called Sundiata. He brought together the **clans** and rulers of western Africa as a single empire in around 1235 CE. Within 100 years the Mali Empire controlled trade in the whole region and stretched around 1,250 miles (2,000 kilometers) across western Africa. As well as trade, the Mali Empire created important centres of learning and religion. Many important **mosques** were built during this time, including the Great Mosque at Djenne—the largest mud-brick building in the world.

The Great Mosque at Djenne was built around the 1200s but was later destroyed. This new version of the mosque was built in the early 1900s.

MANSA MUSA

Mansa Musa ruled the Mali Empire from 1312 to 1337. He was known for his extravagant spending! In 1324 he made a famous **pilgrimage** to Mecca in Saudi Arabia, the holiest place in Islam. He took more than 60,000 people with him, including at least 12,000 **slaves**. He used his wealth to buy luxury goods wherever he went and gave expensive gifts to rulers he met along the way.

Islam and learning

By the time of the Mali Empire, Islam had become the main religion of North and West Africa. It had arrived with traders from the Middle East. The traders also introduced new ideas and knowledge, which they shared with local scholars. Cities such as Timbuktu in Mali soon became important centers of learning as well as trade. By the mid-14th century, Timbuktu had three universities with more than 25,000 students. These included Sankore University, one of the oldest universities in the world, which was partly built under the orders of Mansa Musa.

AFRICA FACT

From the 1300s to the 1500s, Sankore University had more foreign students than New York University does today.

Great Zimbabwe (1100–1500 CE)

Great Zimbabwe was a city and major center of trade in southern Africa. Gold, **ivory**, beads, cloth, and **porcelain** were among the goods it traded with countries as far away as China. At its height, around 18,000 people lived in Great Zimbabwe. At the center of the city was the Great Enclosure, which had thick walls similar to those of European castles. The ruins of Great Zimbabwe can still be seen in modern Zimbabwe today. Great Zimbabwe also gave the modern-day country its name.

This is the Great Enclosure in Great Zimbabwe. It is the largest of the city's many stone structures and is a reminder of the important kingdom that once thrived there.

Kongo (around 1390–1914 CE)

Kongo was one of the largest ancient kingdoms in Central Africa. It was led by a king known as "Manikongo." The Kongo formed close links with Portugal after the Portuguese first came to the region in 1483. These links were so strong that Manikongo and his son were even **baptized** and given the Christian names João and Afonso.

Portuguese settlers were at first welcomed in Kongo, but their role in the Atlantic slave trade (see page 36) meant that the relationship became less friendly. After internal fighting weakened Kongo, it became part of the Portuguese **colony** of Angola in 1914.

A language kingdom

Swahili is a language that developed due to trade between African and Arab peoples along the coastline of eastern Africa. African ivory and gold were exchanged for cloth and spices from the east. As the traders mixed, Arabic words became combined with local Bantu languages. Swahili emerged as a new language. The language gets its name from the Arabic *sawahili*, which means "of the coast."

SOME SWAHILI WORDS

Below are a few common Swahili words that you may have heard:

jambo—hello
safari—journey
asante—thanks
bwana—sir
simba—lion
hakuna matata—no problem.

Daily Life

Much of what we know about ancient Africa comes from the stories of travelers such as Leo Africanus. For some **cultures**, such as the ancient Egyptians or Great Zimbabweans, there are physical remains that also give us clues. Another important type of knowledge is oral history. This is the spoken knowledge that is passed down from one generation to the next. It can teach us a lot about day-to-day life in the past.

LEO AFRICANUS

Leo Africanus was a Spanish Moroccan writer and traveler. He described Timbuktu, in western Africa, around 1510 CE:

"The houses there are very poor, except for those of the king and his nobles. The **merchants** are exceedingly rich and large numbers of black Africans continually come here to buy cloth brought from Barbarie (Morocco) and Europe..."

The riches of power

Power in ancient Africa was often shown by the wealth of its rulers. There are stories of palaces and royal rooms decorated in gold and silk and overflowing with food. Besides the ruler and their protectors and advisers, the court would often include important merchants, scholars, and religious leaders. **Trade** was an important source of wealth, but many rulers also collected **taxes** from their people. Taxes were often paid in the form of crops or cattle rather than as money.

African slavery

Slavery dates back to the ancient Egyptians and was an important trade for many early African kingdoms. Working as a **slave** on the land or in the home of a master was part of everyday life for hundreds of thousands of people. In the Kanem kingdom of western Africa, up to one-third of all people were enslaved. Similar numbers of slaves were found in the kingdoms of Ghana, Mali, and Songhay.

Tribal leaders may not hold much political control in Africa today, but they are still culturally important. This is a Nigerian tribal leader dressed in traditional clothing at a gathering of tribal peoples in Nigeria.

A working life

Most people in ancient Africa spent their days working on the land. They used basic tools, such as an *adze*, or **hoe**, and grew crops to feed their family. In coastal areas and near major rivers, fishing was an important activity. In drier parts of Africa, people kept **livestock** instead of growing **crops**. They would often move with their animals to find water or fresh **pasture**.

Hunting and gathering was another activity for several ancient societies. If people needed things, they would trade their own crops, fish, or livestock for other goods. Markets became important places for people to meet and exchange products. Markets are still important across Africa today, though goods are mainly bought and sold for money now, rather than exchanged.

Staple diets

The main (staple) food eaten by different communities in ancient Africa was linked to what they could grow or trade for in their local area. Different parts of the African **continent** had different specialities. Many of these are still the main staple foods today.

Food type	Description	Where it is found
Couscous	Made from semolina flour (from wheat) and eaten with meat, vegetables, fish, and spicy sauces.	Morocco, Algeria, Tunisia, and other parts of northern Africa.
Yams	A root vegetable that can be boiled, fried, or pounded to make a type of porridge called "fufu."	Across West and Central Africa, but especially popular in Nigeria and Ghana.
Maize	A cereal crop that is roasted (as cobs) or dried and ground into a flour for making porridge or bread.	Throughout sub-Saharan Africa, and a staple food in southern and eastern Africa.

In parts of rural Africa many people still live in family compounds. The women in this village in Burkina Faso paint their compounds with colorful motifs.

Bark cloth

Clothing in ancient Africa was normally made from simple cloth or animal skins. A more unusual fabric used for clothing was bark cloth. In Uganda this was made from the bark of a fig tree. The bark was first stripped and soaked in water to soften it. It could then be hammered flat to make a fabric. In Uganda bark cloth was especially worn by royalty and chiefs during official ceremonies. It was also used to wrap the dead before they were buried. An important chief may be wrapped in up to 200 pieces! Bark cloth is still used in parts of Uganda today.

Skills and crafts

As farming became more organized in early African societies, some people were freed from working the land. They developed new skills and crafts, many of which were linked to materials available in the local area. This gave particular **ethnic groups** a reputation for certain skills or crafts. The Akamba people in Kenya, for example, are known for their skilled drum making. In southern Africa, the Zulu and Ndebele people are famous for their beautiful beadwork.

Working with metal

The Nok culture (500–200 BCE) in Nigeria was one of the earliest known societies to develop skills in ironwork. They used a furnace (oven) to heat up iron ore (rocks containing iron) in order to separate the iron from the rock. The iron could then be shaped into tools for farming, eating, and other uses.

Other ancient societies, such as Great Zimbabwe, also used iron for making tools and weapons. Metalworking was used to make jewelry and objects of art. The treasures of Tutankhamen are one of the most famous examples of this. They show that the ancient Egyptians had developed skills in working with gold. Another culture that showed artistic skill was the Benin kingdom of western Africa. It is especially known for its life-like bronze heads and sculptures, which are often simply called "Benin bronzes."

This Benin bronze shows the face of a lion and is decorated with flowers.

You can find many examples of colorful ceramic pots in markets across Africa today.

Ceramics

Clay is found in many parts of Africa. It has been fired (heated) to make **ceramic** pots and other items since at least 500 BCE. Many ceramic items were made for use in cooking, or for storing and carrying goods such as water and milk. Over time, people developed the skills to make more shaped pieces and decorate them with textures or paints.

27

Trade and Inventions

The ancient Egyptians brought many inventions into the world. They developed digging sticks and **hoes** into an early type of **plow**, for example. Different types of **irrigation** technology were among their most important inventions.

One method of irrigation involved trapping water from the annual flooding of the Nile in specially-dug canals. A mechanism called a *shaduf* was then used to water the fields. A *shaduf* works like a pair of scales with a bucket on one end and a heavy weight on the other. The heavy weight helped to lift the filled bucket so that the water could then be tipped into a channel that took it to the fields.

Building techniques

Buildings in ancient Africa were often quite simple structures. They were made using locally available materials such as mud, sticks, and leaves, and varied in style from region to region. Most people had some skills in simple building techniques.

Larger and more impressive buildings were normally built for kings and leaders, or as religious buildings. The pyramids, Great Zimbabwe, and the early **mosques** in West Africa are examples of this. How the Egyptians built such enormous and mathematically-exact structures as the pyramids, however, is still not known for certain.

Lalibela and the rock-cut churches

Ethiopia is home to some of ancient Africa's most unusual buildings. These are the rock-cut churches in the city of Lalibela. There are 11 churches in total, and they are cut out of solid granite in the ground. They show great skill and craftsmanship, and are thought to have been built by skilled Ethiopian **stonemasons**. Four of these churches—the House of Emmanuel, the House of Mercurios, Abba Libanos, and the House of Gabriel—are carved from one, single piece of rock.

Saint George's Church, in Lalibela, was one of the last rock-cut churches to be built, around 1250 CE. It is carved from rock in the shape of a cross.

Merchants and sellers

Trade has always been part of African life. Trade was often local, but some reached as far away as China. Early kingdoms, such as the Kanem **Empire**, grew strong by controlling trade routes in Africa. The Kanem controlled a large region of West Africa between the 9th and 19th centuries. They became wealthy by demanding payments from traders for safe access through their lands.

Salt was one of the main goods carried by camels. This camel caravan is crossing the salt flats at Lake Assal in Djibouti.

Camel caravans

The trade routes crossing the Sahara Desert to get to Europe or Asia were some of the most important in the ancient world. One of the main ways to transport goods along these routes was by camel. Camels can live for days without food or water, and are used to hot and dry desert conditions. Trade using camels normally involved large groups traveling together. These were known as camel caravans, and could have up to 20,000 camels!

Africa Fact

The giving of gifts was an important part of trade relations for the Kanem-Bornu Empire. On one occasion the king presented the gift of a giraffe to the Sultan of Tunis!

East African trade

Coins found in Zanzibar and Tanzania show that from around 300 CE, East Africa had strong trade links with North Africa, Persia, and India. This trade by sea was closely linked to seasonal winds that blew across the Indian Ocean. Between November and March the winds blew from the east, bringing **merchants** with cloth, spices, and sugar. The merchants would trade their goods for **ivory**, gold, and **slaves**. They would then make their return journey when the winds changed and blew from the west, between April and October.

These traditional sailing boats are known as *dhow* along the coast of East Africa and as *felucca* in Egypt.

Invasion and Exploration

By the 1400s European explorers had heard stories of Africa's great riches, and were becoming interested in exploring the land for their own gain. Africa was also on the European ocean routes to Asia. Stopping along Africa's coast provided a chance to rest and to take on supplies or new **trade**. Over time, Europeans established trading posts on Africa's coast where their ships could habor in safety and store or transfer goods. Contact with Africa made others curious to explore inland from the coast. This led to an age of European exploration that brought Europeans into contact with the **cultures** of ancient Africa. This contact would change Africa forever, and in many ways it marked the end of ancient Africa.

Mungo Park (1771–1806) was a Scottish explorer and one of the first Europeans to travel in West Africa. This sketch shows him coming across a lion.

European settlements

The first Europeans to settle in Africa were the Portuguese and Dutch. The Portuguese had small coastal settlements in what are now Angola and Mozambique. The Dutch settled in South Africa in 1652, where they founded what is now the city of Cape Town. The first settlers were farmers and became known as *boers*, which means "farmer" in the Dutch language. They provided food for ships on their way to India. Later, the Dutch settlers called themselves *Afrikaners* ("Africans") and this term is still used by their descendants today.

CETSHWAYO, THE ZULU WARRIOR

Cetshwayo was a Zulu **warrior** who defeated the British army when they tried to take control of Zululand in January 1879. In July 1879 the British returned and this time captured Zululand from Cetshwayo. In 1882 Cetshwayo traveled to London to ask Queen Victoria for the return of his Zulu kingdom. He was granted his wish, but his powers as king were greatly reduced. When he returned, Zululand was in civil war. Cetshwayo himself died in 1884, marking the end of the Zulu kingdom.

This photograph of Cetshwayo, the Zulu warrior, was taken in 1880.

The beginnings of the slave trade

Slavery had been part of African life for centuries. **Slaves** were traded by many of Africa's early kingdoms.

East African slavery

By the 1700s, slavery was a major trade on the East African coast, with slaves sold to work in the Middle East and Asia. Brazilian traders also took slaves from East Africa, and the French bought slaves for their sugar and coffee **plantations** on the islands of Mauritius and Réunion. This early trade in slaves was controlled by Arabs and Africans. Zanzibar and Mombasa became major centres for the slave trade.

Slave traders

African slave traders would travel with small private armies and raid villages to capture people to sell as slaves. Sometimes these slave traders were working for African rulers. Tippu Tip, for example, was a famous slave trader who worked for the Sultans of Zanzibar. Other slave traders were private businessmen who became very wealthy.

Once they were captured, slaves would normally be chained together using metal chains or ropes. These were attached to wooden boards around the necks of the slaves. The slave trade took place in markets, like other trades. Some slaves would not survive the journey to market and others were so weak by the time they got there, that they sold for a very low price.

TIPPU TIP (1837—1905)

Tippu Tip, or Muhammed Bin Hamid, was born on the island of Zanzibar to an Arab mother and African father. He built a trading empire on the African mainland, dealing mainly in ivory and slaves. His men controlled an area that stretched more than 620 miles (1,000 kilometers) inland from the coast of Tanzania. Tippu Tip also owned large plantations on Zanzibar that grew cloves—a valuable spice that is still grown there today.

Tippu Tip had around 10,000 slaves working for him on his plantations.

Slavery and Colonialism

In the mid-1400s, the **slave trade** in West Africa began to be controlled by European traders.

The Portuguese began to take slaves to work in their new **colonies** in South America. Then, in 1518, the Spanish began to transport slaves to their new colonies in the Caribbean Islands. Soon the French, British, and Dutch also became involved. Each nation used different trading posts along the West African coast to buy slaves and ship them to the Americas. There they would be sold to work on European-owned **plantations** growing sugar, cotton, tobacco, coffee, and other **crops**. These goods were then shipped back to Europe on the empty slave ships.

The transatlantic slave trade had a major impact on the population of Africa. By the mid-19th century, at least 12 million Africans had been captured and transported as slaves. Most ended up on the islands of the Caribbean or in Brazil. Around five per cent were sold into slavery in North America, mostly into what are now the southern United States. Slaves were treated as less human than their white slave owners and lived in miserable conditions.

The European slave trade crossed the Atlantic Ocean from Europe to Africa and then to America.

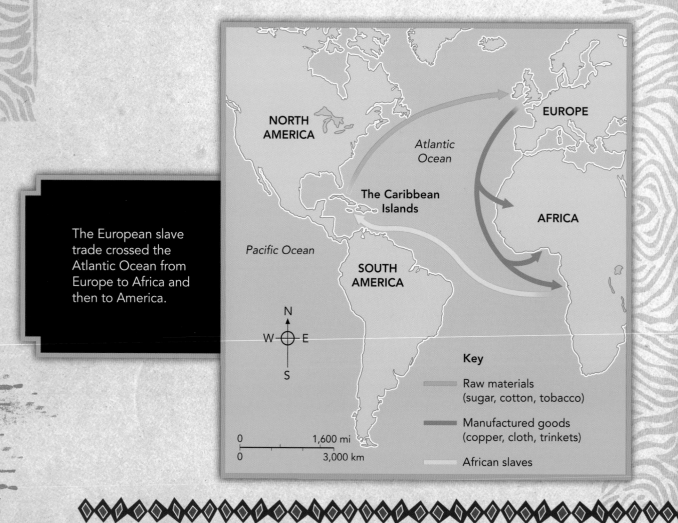

NORTH AMERICA

EUROPE

Atlantic Ocean

The Caribbean Islands

AFRICA

Pacific Ocean

SOUTH AMERICA

N
W—E
S

Key

Raw materials (sugar, cotton, tobacco)

Manufactured goods (copper, cloth, trinkets)

African slaves

0   1,600 mi
0   3,000 km

Surviving the Middle Passage

The Middle Passage was the name given to the 4,000-mile (6,500 kilometer) journey from Africa to the Americas. This could take up to three months, and slaves lived in terrible conditions. Up to 20 per cent of them died on the journey.

The former slave Olaudah Equiano spoke about the conditions on his journey. He said:

"I became so sick … I was not able to eat, nor had I the least desire to taste anything. I now wished for … death, to relieve me; but soon, to my grief, two of the white men offered me eatables; and on my refusing to eat, one of them … laid me across I think the windlass, and tied my feet, while the other whipped me severely."

Olaudah Equiano was a former slave. He earned enough money to buy his freedom, and spent the next 20 years traveling the world.

The end of slavery

Not everyone in Europe was in favor of the slave trade. By the late-1700s a campaign to end slavery had begun in Britain, led by **abolitionists** such as William Wilberforce. There were several reasons for this. Machines had been invented that could work more efficiently than slaves. Britain had also lost its American colonies during the American War of Independence in 1776. This meant it no longer directly benefited from the slave plantations in the Americas.

In 1807 the British government banned slave trading, and from 1834 it became **illegal** to own slaves. Other European nations were slower to give up slavery, and slavery in Europe did not finally end until the early part of the 1900s. In the United States, slavery became illegal in 1865.

Many former slaves continued to live hard lives after slavery ended. These people are working on an American plantation in 1895.

This image shows members of the Liberian government in 1893. The government was mostly made up of freed African American slaves who returned to Liberia when it was given its freedom.

Early African colony

Sierra Leone is a country that was created by the end of slavery. It welcomed freed slaves from the former British colonies in the Americas starting in 1792. The former slaves settled in an area that became called Freetown. Freetown is still the capital of Sierra Leone today and is a reminder of the origins of the country. In 1808 Freetown was made a colony of the British Empire, one of the first European colonies in Africa.

A weakened land

Four hundred years of slavery had greatly weakened African societies. Kingdoms that had once been strong became weak and vulnerable. There was an increase in fighting between communities that had once lived happily together and this further weakened them. This meant that when the Europeans arrived to **colonize** parts of Africa, many societies were simply too weak to resist them.

The Scramble for Africa

At first, Europeans had little interest in governing Africa. They were more interested in trading goods such as **ivory**, spices, gold, and slaves. As more countries became interested in this trade, however, nations began to protect their trade by taking control of parts of the **continent**. The discovery of valuable **resources**, such as gold and diamonds in South Africa and copper in Zambia, made these pressures even greater. Soon, European nations were desperately competing to control as much of the continent as possible. This became known as the "Scramble for Africa." Little attention was paid by the European powers to the interests of the African people.

Berlin Conference

In 1884 the 14 countries that already had interests in Africa were invited to a special conference in Berlin. The meeting was to agree trade rules and colonial boundaries in Africa. Not a single African was at the meeting! By the end of the conference, Africa had been divided into 50 new colonies. The boundaries of these colonies were drawn with no thought for existing African societies. Some were simply straight lines on a map that divided entire **cultures**.

This cartoon about the Berlin Conference of 1884 shows the European leaders "cutting up" Africa as if it were a large cake.

Cecil Rhodes of Britain was one of the most famous of Africa's colonists. He was prime minister of the Cape Colony in South Africa, and he started the De Beers diamond-mining company, which is still around today.

Changed forever

European colonialism in Africa lasted in most parts of the continent for less than 100 years, but it changed many countries enormously. New languages and religions were introduced. Land was taken and local cultures were destroyed. But despite all these changes and the effects that continue today, it is important to remember that Africa has its own pre-colonial history—a history that is richer and older than almost any other on Earth.

Timeline

3.5 million years ago   Very early **ancestors** begin to walk in the upright position.

1.6 million years ago   The human ancestor *Homo habilis* is living in Africa.

170,000 BCE   *Homo sapiens* evolve in East Africa, spreading throughout the **continent** and globe.

3000 BCE –670 BCE   Ancient Egyptians live around the floodplains of the Nile Delta.

715 BCE   Kushites from neighboring Nubia conquer Egypt and rule until 662 BCE.

500–200 BCE   Nok society uses iron to create tools.

300–1100 CE   Kingdom of ancient Ghana is an important center of **trade**, skilled crafts, and learning.

1100–1500   Great Zimbabwe is a city and major center of trade in southern Africa.

1235   Mali Empire begins to spread across West Africa under the rule of Sundiata.

1324   Mansa Musa, a ruler of the Mali Empire, makes a pilgrimage to Mecca in Saudi Arabia, taking 60,000 people with him.

1390–1914   The Kongo kingdom is strong and has links with Portugal for many years.

1652   Dutch settlers found the city of Cape Town in what is now South Africa.

1799   The Rosetta Stone is found, with writings in Egyptian **hieroglyphics** and Greek, allowing experts to begin decoding and understanding Egyptian writings.

1795   The British land at the Cape of Good Hope.

1807–1860   The transatlantic **slave** trade ends after 400 years and around 12 million people being shipped from Africa to the Americas.

1865   Slavery ends in the United States at the end of the Civil War.

1879   The British-Zulu War is fought between the British Empire and the Zulu Empire.

1884   European nations meet at the Berlin Conference to divide Africa into **colonies**, and agree trade rules concerning the continent.

1922   The ancient Egyptian **tomb** of Tutankhamen is discovered in the Valley of the Kings.

1959   Mary and Louis Leakey find ancient remains at Olduvai Gorge in Tanzania.

1990–2003   The Human Genome Project uses DNA research to find out more about the origins of humans.

Glossary

abolitionist person who supported the ending of slavery

ancestor family member who has died a long time ago

baptize perform the ceremony of baptism, by which a person becomes a member of the Christian faith

ceramic object made of clay which has been hardened by being baked in an oven

charcoal fuel made from burned wood

chariot two-wheeled horse-drawn carriage used in battle

civilization society with a high level of art, science, and government

clan large group of families who are related to one another

colonize make another country a colony of your own country

colony land controlled by another country

continent one of the main areas of land on Earth. Many countries may be found in one continent.

crop plant grown for use by people, such as cereals or vegetables

culture actions and beliefs of a society

DNA deoxyribonucleic acid; material found in each living cell that contains instructions on how that cell should behave and function

empire nation that is responsible for ruling several countries at once

engineering the application of scientific and mathematical knowledge in order to find solutions to practical problems such as building, construction, and mining

ethnic group people who share a culture and language

evolve develop certain qualities or characteristics through generations of offspring

fertile rich in materials or health needed for growth

fossil plant or animal whose remains have been preserved or have left a record in rock

hieroglyphics system of recording information using symbols and pictures known as hieroglyphs

hoe tool with a flat blade and a long handle used for planting, weeding, and gardening

illegal against the law

irrigation the bringing of water to crops and fields by digging ditches, laying pipes, or through other means

ivory material that comes from animal tusks, especially those of elephants

livestock animals kept for use or profit, such as farm animals

merchant person who buys and sells goods

migrate to move from one country or region and settle in another

mineral nonorganic natural substances found in the earth

mosque place of worship for Muslims

mummification process by which a dead body is preserved by embalming, drying, and wrapping it in cloth

pasture farmland which is used for feeding animals, such as cows and sheep, rather than growing crops

pharaoh ancient Egyptian ruler

pilgrimage journey to a place of religious worship

plantation large farm where crops are grown in huge quantities by people who live and work there

plow turn over soil in preparation for planting crops

porcelain fine, hard, thin ceramic

preserve to prevent from decaying

primitive basic; in an early stage of development

rainforest thick, forested area in a tropical region which supports a huge diversity of plant and animal life

resource mineral or raw material that is used in industry, business, and government to produce goods or services

slave person who is forced to work for another

species particular type of animal or plant

stonemason person who is skilled in using stone to make buildings

tax money that the government collects from people and businesses in order to finance the running of the country

tomb place where a person is buried

trade buy and sell goods

turban long piece of cloth wound round the head

warrior person engaged in a battle or fighting for a particular cause

45

Find Out More

Books

Barr, Gary. *History and Activities of the West African Kingdoms.* Chicago, Ill.: Heinemann Library, 2007.

Bowden, Rob. *Africa South of the Saraha.* Chicago, Ill.: Heinemann Library, 2008.

Ganeri, Anita. *Ancient Egyptians.* Minneapolis, Minn.: Compass Point Books, 2007.

Shuter, Jane. *Ancient West African Kingdoms.* Chicago, Ill.: Heinemann Library, 2009.

Woods, Michael and Mary B. *Seven Wonders of Ancient Africa.* Minneapolis, Minn.: Twenty-First Century Books, 2008.

Websites

BBC World Service
www.bbc.co.uk/worldservice/africa/features/storyofafrica
This site explains the history of Africa and its people.

Kidipede
www.historyforkids.org/learn/africa
This website for children describes many different aspects of ancient Africa.

Smithsonian
http://www.si.edu/Encyclopedia_SI/History_and_Culture/Africa_History.htm
Use this site to find out all you want to know about African history and art.

Places to visit

Many museums have good collections of African art and **culture**. Here are some examples:

Museum for African Art
36-01 43rd Avenue at 36th Street
Long Island City, NY 11101
Tel: (718) 784-7700
www.africanart.org

National Museum of African Art
Smithsonian Institution
950 Independence Avenue, SW
Washington, DC 20560
Tel: (202) 633-4600
http://africa.si.edu

The Field Museum
1400 S. Lake Shore Drive
Chicago, IL 60605
Tel: (312) 922-9410
www.fieldmuseum.org

Index